Dedication

Thanks to Linda Markowitz and Steve West, whose patience and generosity taught me the art of guerrilla garage sailing.

—Diana

To our mom, who managed fabulously as a single parent raising five kids, with the help of a few good garage sales.

—Monica

Contents

Introduction

Garage Sales *are* fabulous. There are hundreds of thousands of people across this country that enjoy hunting for useful items at Garage Sales. There are friends that like to spend time together seeking vintage fashions in other people's backyards nearly every weekend. There are grandparents that are looking for bargains for their grandkids, home improvement buffs that like to find tools, collectors that like salt and pepper shakers, kids that like baseball cards and families looking to stretch their budgets by purchasing used furniture. Some people love Garage Sales because they just love Garage Sales!

These countless thousands of people are cruising around looking for Garage Sales. We call people who cruise for sales *Garage Sailors*. (This is our term for people who attend Garage Sales—a variation on Garage Salers.) Garage Sailors have cash in hand and are happy to spend it in your port—provided they know about your sale and can find you. Your job is to make it easy for them to find your sale, and to have the merchandise ready so they can give you their money and take away the stuff you've accumulated and don't want anymore. Sounds like a pretty good situation doesn't it?

If you've wanted to have a Garage Sale but didn't have the time to plan it, or didn't know how—you now have a kit that will help to make it easy. If you are experienced at conducting sales, you'll find the worksheets and signs

included in this kit will help you get the job done easily, in less time and with more fun and profit.

We've thoroughly researched Garage Sales as a serious business proposition and have included many professional ideas from marketing, advertising, design and display that work for small businesses—which is what a Garage Sale really is—if only for a weekend.

It isn't necessary to use everything here to have a successful sale, but even one or two of our ideas may bring more customers or more sales per customer—and therefore more money.

Occasionally Garage Sales are necessary for difficult reasons, such as the death of a loved one. We hope that, even in trying circumstances, this kit helps makes the process of conducting a Garage Sale easier and more profitable.

We're interested in knowing how your sale goes and in hearing any ideas you have for improving future editions of this kit. At the back of the book you'll find our address so you can write to us. We'll appreciate the feedback and so will the future readers of this book. Thank you, good luck, and may many Garage Sailors cruise to your port!

Diana Rix & Monica Rix Paxson, "The Garage Sale Sisters"

Note: The term "Garage Sale" is generic. It is understood by people everywhere to mean the sale of household goods and clothing, conducted by an individual or group of non-professionals at a residence. Other names are occasionally used to better describe the location of sale (yard sale, patio sale, basement sale) or some other attribute of the sale (moving sale, tag sale). However, Garage Sale is the most common and universally understood term. This is why advertising for all other names is grouped under the "Garage Sale" heading in newspaper classified sections throughout the country. So, no matter where you hold your sale or what you call it, this book will help you.

Getting Started

This kit is designed to provide you with the information you need to carry out a successful garage sale. It's created to help you plan and conduct a garage sale rather than researching how to do it. Here's the practical help you need to do it.

If you are like us, your time is limited. The less on the to-do list, the better we like it. We've designed this book to help you plan, advertise, set up, and conduct a sensational event very easily. Here's how:

- The worksheets and forms that follow this text will help you stay organized. The ◆ symbol appearing in the text indicates the worksheet or form discussed in the text appears in the Appendix at the end of the book.

- Ads, invitations, signs and flyers will ensure that you have good attendance. These are also indicated by a ◆ symbol.

- Sales, display and pricing tips will help you make money.

- People that share in your sale with you will make it fun, offer you additional merchandise, help you out while preparing, setting up and conducting the sale.

This book is designed for you to take notes as you are reading it. You'll understand why when you realize how

many ideas you'll have as you think about the various aspects of holding a sale. The suggestion here is to *write ideas down.* If you think of something to sell, something to do, someone to invite, another place to put up a flyer or advertise, write it down immediately as you are reading this book.

The column on the right hand side of the page is reserved for your notes. You'll also find specific questions there that we hope will trigger ideas.

Taking notes will accomplish several things—

- You may not be able to remember everything later.

- You'll have a head start on completing the worksheets that are a part of this kit.

- You'll be able to check things off as they are accomplished.

- You will tend to be less overwhelmed if you commit your thoughts to paper. You can avoid the anxiety and stress of a large project by not trying to carry the list of things you want to do around in your head.

This could be fun.

This could be a party!

This could be a Fabulous Money-Making Garage Sale!

Scheduling

Give yourself plenty of time to plan and prepare. While this book will make the organizing more efficient, you will need to plan the sale for a date far enough in advance to give you adequate time to round up and prepare all the items you wish to sell.

Inviting people and advertising, which we'll begin planning next, also require time. We recommend giving yourself *at least* two weeks to prepare for your sale.

Two weeks should be adequate time to prepare for *most* sales, but this will depend on individual circumstances. For example, some areas require permits. A call to your city, town hall or other local governmental office should help. While in most areas this isn't a concern, it shows the need for planning. The goal is to pull off a polished sale, not one that looks like it was just thrown together at the last moment.

If your life is complicated or you like moving at a leisurely pace, take an extra two weeks. Give yourself the time to do it right. It will pay off.

Weekends are the best days to have your sale, preferably not the weekend of a holiday. Check your calendar to make sure nothing else important is scheduled. Three day sales are common, (Friday, Saturday, and Sunday) but for the kind of well-orchestrated sale planned here, one day may be sufficient. Garage sale folklore wisdom is evenly

Does my community require a permit for a Garage Sale?

What other major weekend events are coming up for me or my family members?

for my community?

My Garage Sale will be held on:

The rain date is:

divided on the merits of either Saturday or Sunday. It's a toss up.

You'll probably want to have your sale for two days to give yourself ample opportunity to sell everything.

Be forewarned: often second days bring only half the receipts of the first.

You may want to schedule a "rain date" for the following weekend. We recommend this if you live in a climate where rainy weather is common and your sale is outdoors. If you want to schedule a rain date, you'll need to set the date where two subsequent weekends are free non-holiday weekends.

Invite Everyone

Our three main objectives are to make having a garage sale profitable, easy and fun. Easy and fun means doing it with other people. Now that you have the dates set, you can begin to invite them.

Remember, garage sales are *social* events. Involve other people from the beginning: your neighbors, friends, co-workers, and kids. The simplest reasons for doing this is to attract more people to your sale. It's a law of human nature that people attract people, and groups of people draw crowds.

Having more people involved in the sale also means more *merchandise*, which is the number one way to attract customers. Neighbors on your block or in your apartment or condo complex are logical people to include. After all, they won't have far to move their merchandise to your home or some other common area. Their items can be distinguished from yours by using different colored price tags (or different colored markers on masking tape or stickers). But don't stop there. Invite your friends and co-workers to join in the sale too.

You might consider asking your neighbors to hold sales at their own homes at the same time as yours. Some communities have block clubs that can help to organize such events. Most people are responsive to a good plan if there is someone who will take on the leadership involved in

Who would I like to hold this sale with?

Who do I know with a lot of junk?

Which of my neighbors might also like to have a sale?

It would be fun to have these people there:

The people who like to help out are:

The people who owe me big-time favors are:

setting a date and organizing the promotion. We recommend that you consider taking the project on. It won't add significantly to the time or expense of holding a sale and may generate more buyers. In any case, if nearby neighbors are holding sales at the same time, consider it help—not competition. It would be hard to imagine a buyer stopping to browse at your neighbor's sale without checking yours as well.

Collaborating means extra pairs of hands and whole new networks of potential customers. When it comes to having a garage sale, the more the merrier. Having others join you will increase the attention your sale receives and will cut your costs in placing ads.

If you are advertising for multiple sellers, make sure you discuss the anticipated expenses with each seller and have an agreement about how you will be reimbursed. We suggest that you collect money from each seller at the time the ads are placed. This avoids problems if a participant backs out at a future date. Having a seller write you a check for advertising costs will demonstrate that they are seriously committed to joining in. If neighbors or other sellers are joining in, make sure to note that in the ad.

In addition to being more profitable, sales involving neighbors, friends and family are more fun! You will appreciate plenty of helpers, but don't think of it as having to ask people to help you with your sale. Think about who you would like to have share the experience with you. Your garage sale can be an event everyone enjoys and remembers fondly.

If you feel awkward asking friends and neighbors to join in, you may find it easier to make a specific request. "Would you come over Saturday morning to help me set up? Would you relieve me as Cashier on Sunday afternoon?" The **Invitation Worksheet** ◆ will help you organize your efforts in enrolling others to help or participate in your Garage Sale.

We recommend that you use the opportunity to make your Garage Sale a party. Get to know your neighbors. Challenge your friends to bring their fashion mistakes. Dress your kids like clowns! Give lollypops to children. Give lollypops to grown-ups! Throw an old 78 on the victrola and dance in the driveway. Have a good time!

Which brings us to the camera, or videocam if you prefer. Make sure you have plenty of film, fresh batteries, and an official camera person to record the event. Your garage sale should be recorded for the future! Make sure to get shots of the people and house "before," "during," and "after" your sale. Don't worry, you'll be too wrapped up in helping the customers to notice the camera and you'll get lots of great candid shots of everyone involved. Your camera person needs to hold onto their equipment to avoid its being sold or stolen. Consider making extra prints as gifts for the people that helped.

Who likes to take pictures or use the video camera?

Selecting the Location

Where is the most visible place to hold my sale?

Where will I store unsold items securely over night?

While a garage can be a great location for a garage sale, it is only one of many. Other locations, like a patio, yard, porch, or basement, all have their own advantages. A high-rise resident may be able to use a building party room or their own apartment.

The term Garage Sale has come to be a generic term encompassing a variety of site locations. If your sale is not in an actual garage, you can avoid any confusion by placing signs in the yard to direct people to the actual location. If you have a doorman, make sure to give them instructions on how to receive your "guests" and where to direct them.

The garage sale signs included in this kit may be modified by adding specific locations. The location will depend on your own particular requirements and some general considerations: size, convenience, visibility, and weather conditions.

The most important consideration in planning your sale is convenience. Merchandise already in or near the garage is more easily secured at night. That is certainly easier than hauling everything in from the yard at night and out again for the next day of the sale.

The visibility of the location *is very* important to your customers. Visibility goes beyond making sure customers know how to find your residence. It involves having your merchandise visibly inviting to those who drive by. Front yard sales are often a better idea than back yard sales because visible merchandise attracts like no other advertising can.

Please check to find out if your community has any specific rules about where sales can be held. A call to your city or town hall may save you from embarrassment. Some communities are very strict about permits and locations while others have no regulations.

While deciding on a location you should make arrangements for parking. If neighbors object to letting your customers park in front of their property you will want to post **No Parking** or **Park Here** signs ◆ on the day of the sale.

One of the best ways to ensure your next door neighbor's cooperation is to invite them to join in. However, even if you are not comfortable with doing that, it is usually a good idea to let them know about the sale in advance. Hand them an **Invitation** ◆ or drop it in their mailbox. Give them an opportunity to voice any considerations *before* the sale. Many problems can be worked out in advance with even the most difficult of neighbors. You want to avoid dealing with problems during the sale by giving your neighbors advance notice.

Is customer parking likely to create problems for my neighbors?

What neighbors do I want to invite to the sale?

Advertising

Where are the best places to advertise Garage Sales in my community?

To make the most of your sale you will need to advertise it. For maximum results you will want to use word-of-mouth, newspaper, neighborhood and point of sale advertising. Advertising is not a place to cut corners. Ads need to be well-planned and thought out to stir up the interest that makes a sale a success.

Contact your local papers well ahead of time to have information on ad rates, categories, deadlines and numbers of words sent to you. You should begin proceeding with the following steps at least two weeks prior to your sale.

Classified Ads

Classified ads are the way most people will get news of your sale unless you live in a very small community. Designing your classified ad and seeing that arrangements are made for running it are probably the most critical steps in preparing for your sale. Use the **Advertising Worksheet** ◆ while writing, and preparing to run, your classified ad.

You'll reach more people for the buck through an ad in your local daily newspaper than in any other way. Weekly newspapers can also be very effective since people tend to use them to find ways to spend their leisure time. Shopping circulars, which tend to be almost exclusively classified ads, can also be an inexpensive way of reaching people in your area. What paper would you look in to find out about Garage Sales? Some communities have only

one option. Some have several. If you aren't sure which is best, ask a number of friends or neighbors in your area. You may be able to budget ads in more than one paper.

Check with your local newspapers to confirm when your ad must be placed and paid for in order for it to run on the days you want. We recommend that you either place your ad by phone or personally drop it off at the newspaper's office. Some papers require that ad copy be mailed and some require that payment be made upon placement, so you'll need to plan accordingly. Make sure you fulfill *all* the newspaper's requirements. It would be a shame to be all ready for a sale and then discover that the newspaper failed to run your ad. You may want to get a copy of the paper to make sure your ad appears and to verify its contents.

Ads placed in weekly newspapers should come out the week before and/or the week of your sale. In the daily newspaper(s), your ad should begin running the day before your sale and continue through the days it is in progress. If you have scheduled your sale for a Friday, Saturday and Sunday, your ads should begin on Thursday and run through Sunday. You should also take note of the following considerations as you decide when to run your ads.

- Dedicated Garage Sailors are said to consider Thursday's paper their primary guide, but no one that serious could be expected to miss Friday's ads either.

- The day the food ads come out (either Wednesday or Thursday depending on the paper) is the day with the highest circulation. You should seriously consider extending your ad to include this issue.

- Saturday typically has the lowest circulation, but that is generally not true among people

What daily newspaper is it important for me to advertise in?

Which days?

What weekly newspaper should I advertise in?

What shopping circulars are distributed in my area?

looking for garage sales. Saturday is a must if your sale runs Saturday and/or Sunday.

- Discount rates for a week often make 7 days of advertising the better bargain.

A good way to see what works in your community is to ask people who have already run garage sales, and to ask the advertising department of the different papers.

Designing Your Ads

Ads have to be written to attract attention. They must include information on when and where your sale is to be held, but they must also give people a reason for *wanting* to attend. Your ad must *create* interest. The only information that it is mandatory to include in your ad are the days of the sale and your address. We will assemble the rest of your ad by first considering some 'optional' information you may want to include, and then crafting the final touches that are necessary for maximum impact.

Time of the Sale

You may want to include the time of your sale. If you state only the days, most people will assume it is from dawn to dusk and arrive accordingly. If you think that including the times of the sale will solve the problem of people arriving at dawn, be forewarned: arrivals will begin at *least* an hour before the sale is scheduled to begin and maybe more. If your ad states 9–5, people will arrive at 8:00 am or before.

One strategy is to list the starting time as an hour later than you really intend to begin, so that you will be ready when people arrive. Commonly, people try to solve this problem by including in their ad the caution "No Early Birds". This is often included in ads that don't state a starting time, leaving it up to the Garage Sailor to decide what is early.

What time do I want to begin my sale?

What will I advertise as the starting time?

We think it is best to set a time and then stick to it. You'll feel pressured to start earlier but you can simply not answer the door. We've included a sign **Sale Begins** ◆ making a polite request that the doorbell not be rung before the scheduled starting time to help you with this issue. Overly zealous Garage Sailors are occasionally a nuisance. Don't leave it up to chance unless you plan to receive people as early as 6:00 am.

In any event you should probably expect to have arrivals before you are prepared, and you should decide ahead of time how you will handle them. You may want to cord off the entrance to your yard or put a sign on the gate if you'll be in the yard setting up. It is annoying to have to fend off early arrivals at a time when you have so much to do and think about, so don't feel obligated to offer lengthy explanations. If possible, it's a good idea to assign someone to hold them off for you. Remember, getting into the sale early is a game that veteran Garage Sailors play. They really won't be offended if you stand up to them. You are the boss here!

The problem of having people arrive after you have closed down for the day can be solved by posting the **Garage Sale Closed** ◆ or **Come Back Tomorrow** ◆ signs included in this kit. You may want to announce the closing five minutes before you close for the day to allow people to make their final selections and pay for them.

Rain Dates
If weather is a concern you may want to inform people that your sale will be held "same time next week if it rains" or "rain or shine." We've included a **Sorry—We were Rained Out. Please Come Back Next Week** ◆ sign to hang on the door if it is needed.

How will I handle early arrivals?

Will I advertise my phone number?

Phone Number

Including your phone number in the ad encourages people to call and ask about what you have to sell. People will call to inquire about particular items listed in your ad or to ask "what do you have for sale?" If you are willing to sell things before your sale or to tell people specifically what you will have available, including your phone number is a good idea. If you want people to come and find out for themselves, and to limit sales to the actual garage sale, don't include your phone number.

Amazingly, people will call and ask you questions that are clearly answered in the ad: what's the address? what time do you start? It may simply be human nature, or maybe some people routinely call before going anywhere, but if you are aggravated by such questions, avoid printing your phone number.

The Hook

At this point your ad includes the actual days it will be held, your address, and the optional information (time, rain date and phone number) that you've decided to include. Now it's time to decide what else to include to catch your reader's interest. In advertising, this is called "the hook." The hook is what will hook the reader's attention and lure them to your sale. We need to examine what Garage Sailors want to see and make sure to include that in your ads.

One of the most common ways of attracting people through garage sale ads is to include mention of what you will have for sale. You may list particular items that you think will attract buyers: an oriental carpet, a set of sterling silver flatware, a stereo, or bicycle. One or two particularly desirable items shown in the ad will generate the crowds that help ensure other items sell. Also effective are references to categories of goods, like toys or furniture. Below is a list of items that are frequently fast movers at

garage sales. If you will have some of these items in your sale you may want to include them in your ad:

List of Best Sellers

furniture
books
carpets, rugs
kitchen items
glassware, pottery and dishes
toys
kids clothes
baby equipment and furniture
tools
camping equipment
sports equipment
plants
lamps
vintage jewelry

Other good selling items that make less exciting ad material, should be kept in mind as you collect your wares to sell:

lamp shades
towels and linens
blankets
picture frames
office and school supplies

In addition to mentioning specific items and categories of items, general statements about your merchandise can be very effective. Consider the following:

Everything Under the Sun
Everything From 25 Cents to $100
Treasures of Three Families
Multi-Household
Must See to Believe
Items Too Numerous to List
20 Year Collection of Junk

What best selling items do I have to sell?

GARAGE SALE

What collectible items do I have to sell?

Gobs and Gobs of Goodies
Something for Everyone
Unbelievable Bargains
Amazing Bargains
Bargains Galore
Prices Slashed — Must Sell This Weekend
Collectibles/Treasures
Fantastic Finds
You Want It, We've Got It
Multitudes of Misc.
Huge Assortment
Giant Selection
Sacrifice Due to Job Transfer

You can also include statements about the sale itself:

The Mother of All Garage Sales
GONGA GARAGE SALE
Reformed Pack Rat Cleans Out
Family Household for Three Generations
The Eclectic Garage Sale
Mama's Basement Sale of the Century
Traditional American Farm Family Barn Sale
Out with the 50s, In with the 90s Garage Sale
Gigantic Garage Sale
Fabulous Neighborhood Garage Sale
Rummage Extravaganza

What's my hook?

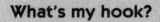

According to the experts on marketing small businesses, psychologists have determined that the words having the most power to persuade people are: you, money, easy, safety, save, new, results, health, love, discovery, free, proven, and guarantee. We'd also like to suggest our list of the most persuasive words to describe garage sales: bargains, huge, everything, treasure.

New Discovery: Boxes of Bargains
Do You Love Treasure?
Proven Money-Saver: Our Garage Sale

Ad writing needs to be taken seriously, but you can have fun doing it. The selection of a few words can make an important impression. The best ads are creative and fun, they prepare customers for an exciting sale and bring them expecting to buy.

Another technique might be to announce that you will have *free* coffee at your sale. Obviously refreshments can be sold for profit and we'll be talking later about concession stands. But providing some free refreshments can also be an effective advertising technique increasing the overall profitability of your sale.

Our kit provides you with an **Advertising Worksheet** ◆ to help you write copy for you to submit to your local newspapers. You'll also find an **Ad Placement Request** ◆ ready to fill out and be mailed if that's your newspaper's policy.

Word-of-Mouth Advertising

After setting a date, you'll immediately want to let others know about the sale. Advertising is only one way of doing this. You are the best promoter possible for your sale! Hand *everyone* you know an **Invitation** ◆. When you get started you'll understand why we recommend inviting everyone. You'll be amazed at how many people like garage sales—both women and men.

Extend a warm personal invitation as you hand an invitation to your co-workers, the kid's teachers, other parents, the folks at your church or synagogue, health club or other organizations. You'll get lots of smiles and many people will follow through on the invitation.

If only your own items are being sold, you may want to consider extending a small discount (which can be printed on the invitation) to your close contacts.

These are the friends I want to invite:

These are the co-workers I want to invite:

Invite people to invite their friends. Encourage them to invite people you mutually know. "Aunt Em, will you be sure to invite your neighbor Mrs. Wilbur? I think she might enjoy this."

Flyers

You'll need a bunch of **Flyers** ◆ to post on bulletin boards. We've provided one as part of this kit, but you will need to photocopy more. Give your spouse, friends, neighbors, and relatives copies of flyers to post for you. Take them with you everywhere. Take thumbtacks or a stapler too. Put them up on bulletin boards wherever you can. Post them at grocery stores, churches, laundromats, libraries and work or school cafeterias. Tack them to phone poles at bus stops. Put them anywhere people gather. This is the simplest, and most often neglected form of advertising. The extra bit of effort you are making will generate more customers and more profits for you.

Neighborhood Advertising

We've provided signs for you to photocopy and post around your neighborhood. Remember to take tape, stapler and tacks with you on your sign posting mission. Wooden stakes purchased at hardware stores or lumber yards may be appropriate in some locations. Telephone poles, light poles, and trees are potential posting places. You can post signs up to a week before the sale. Any longer is unnecessary and may be counterproductive. Your community may have specific regulations on signs.

Don't forget in front of your own house! The weekend before your sale you can post a sign in front of your residence to notify people of your upcoming sale. We've included a **Garage Sale Here** ◆ sign for that purpose. If your garage faces an alley, post one that's visible from the

GARAGE SALE

alley as well. This will catch the interest of neighbors and passers-by, reminding them to return for your sale.

Now for a truly unique idea: Garage Sale signs on your car! Why not? We'd suggest they be taped (one on each side) onto the car doors to avoid interfering with visibility. Use masking or artists' tape to tape them on—anything that won't damage the paint. Be sure to take them off after the sale. You'll be advertising your sale as you drive around your neighborhood. Forget any reluctance you may have about making a fool of yourself: this is just good business. People will probably congratulate you on your good marketing sense.

Early on the morning of the sale (or the night before) post signs to direct people from nearby streets. These signs should be placed at major intersections within a six block radius of the sale. **Direction Arrows ◆** should be placed on signs to indicate the direction of the sale and follow-up arrow signs should be placed at any intersections along the route where a turn is necessary, or to simply indicate that the driver should continue proceeding straight ahead. We've included a **Sign Placement Worksheet ◆** to help you plan the number of signs you will need and where they should be placed.

These signs should be well-secured to wooden stakes and telephone poles. Tacks or flat head nails are best. Signs should be well-placed and generously distributed. They are an extremely important part of getting people to your sale. The signs themselves are specially designed to draw attention. Not only will they help guide the Garage Sailor to your sale, the impulse buyer will also respond to an inviting sign. Take special care that their location gives them maximum impact, for example, at the entrance to a shopping center or large grocery store.

Who would help me distribute flyers and invitations?

Here are some great places for signs:

For added impact, you might attach a bunch of balloons to each sign post. This adds a festive touch and will ensure that many more people will read the sign. Balloons are inexpensive and if you have kids, this is something that can get them involved. Make sure the balloons don't interfere with people's ability to read the signs.

Remember that traffic flows in both directions on most streets, so you'll need to plan the arrangement of the signs to make sure that traffic on both sides of the street can see them. Often this will mean a sign on each side of the street.

Please be responsible. When your sale is over, remove all of the signs.

Point-of-Sale Advertising

Point-of-sale advertising is designed to spark the browser's interest during the sale. A table of wares that might in normal circumstances attract little attention, will occupy hordes of bargain seekers if it is topped with our sign saying **Everything on this Table 50¢"** ◆.

On the east coast, Garage Sales are often called Tag Sales. This term is a hold over from the "tag" used to tell the historic lineage of the piece of artwork or antique furniture being sold. Of course, this kind of information is great if you happen to be selling antiques. However, you can certainly use the price tag to give your merchandise an air of distinction.

Who wants an ordinary monopoly game? But pick up the tag and read:

> "Real Estate Mogul Starter Kit—the very kit that launched Donald Trump's career. Contains both Boardwalk and Park Place—rental value alone of over $500 per month. Only $3.00.

We learned the lesson of creativity of this sort from a friend who brought a mother cat and a bunch of kittens back to the United States from Spain where he'd been living for several years. Although the cats were mixed breed, he explained that they were roof cats, not alley cats. In Spain, where the buildings are built against each other, cats roam the roofs, not the alleys. He wasn't able to find someone in Spain to take the whole cat family and wouldn't separate the kittens from their mother prematurely. When the kittens were a bit older he ran an ad in the paper seeking homes for the kittens. He got no response. Until he ran an ad like this:

> Exotic Spanish Roof Cats, bilingual. Free to a good home.

The phone continued to ring long after the last kitten found a home. Several people wanted to know if they were really bilingual.

If you have the time and have a sense of humor, tag some of your merchandise with tiny stories or a bit of information about the item. You'll have fun, the reader will enjoy the silliness and people will hunt around to see what else they can find to read about.

Examples

Stuffed Rabbit	Her name is Bun Bun. She likes snuggles. We thought you should know. $1
Changing Table	Congratulate us. We thought we'd never be getting rid of this. $15
"Hot Dress"	This dress was responsible for our daughter Sarah. Haven't fit in it since. Wear it with caution. You've been warned. $6
Bird Cage	Tweety has been released on parole. $3

My tag ideas:

Typewriter   Has experience on term papers, re-
              sumes and the first three paragraphs of
              the Great American Novel. $18

We will suggest several other point-of-sale advertising
techniques in the section on set-up and display.

Gathering Goods for Sale

In order to gather goods you will need boxes to collect things in.

The More the Better

Heaps of merchandise helps. Obviously, the more things you have to sell, the more you can expect to sell. But the logic of the law 'the more the better' goes beyond the obvious. Not only does more give you more to sell, but more merchandise also increases the chances that you will sell <u>all</u> of your merchandise. Greater quantity (and variety) sparks interest, and sales.

There is another reason for the law "the more, the better." The psychology of the Garage Sailor is that of someone on the hunt. Unlike shoppers at a department store who expect to be able to know where to find what they're looking for, the thrill for the Garage Sailor is in the hunt. The most enthusiastic buyers are those who find their treasure after a prolonged search. The more you give them to search through to find it, the better.

You Can't Tell What Someone Will Buy

We heard a story about a woman who became convinced that people would buy anything when she observed someone purchase a half-used tube of ointment at a Garage Sale. What you think is junk is the next person's treasure. Don't be critical. Get it out there. Sell it. Take the money. Go figure.

I'd be amazed if someone bought my:

What do I really want to get rid of?

What's cluttering up my life?

You can not possibly know what someone will want because the Garage Sailor's hunt is for something even they probably didn't know they were looking for. The greater your wonder at the item's appeal the greater the finder's triumph. Saleable things are those that people either want or need, and you can't guess or explain either. Don't try. Provide as much merchandise as possible, and keep an open mind about what might be saleable. What is a rusted piece of metal to you is a valuable tool, work of art, or vintage farm implement to another. The old trash bleach bottle from your grandmother's basement may complete someone else's collection.

Gathering Goods

Gathering the goods for your sale will not be as easy as it sounds. You will need a dogged determination to collect everything you no longer want or need. Think of the service you're providing: cleaning up your environment and recycling goods! But don't think of it only in terms of getting rid of things, think about the money you'll get in return, and how much more useful that will be. We've included a **Collecting Worksheet** ◆ as a checklist to help survey all areas of your home for items to sell.

Tips:
- Conduct a thorough search of your house, (basement, garage, attic, shed, etc.) putting everything for your sale in boxes. If you haven't used something in the last year, it's garage sale material. Half empty paint cans, scraps of carpet, a single ceiling tile, a broken picture frame, the egg poacher you've never used—take it all!

- Complete your mission with as little contemplation and as much determination as possible. Try to get it over with all at once and don't change your mind or let others change it. Once some-

thing's in the box, keep it there. This holds true for children as well. Small children are all too happy to drag back out an old, long-ignored toy or garment and attach huge emotional significance to it if you make the mistake of showing it to them. If you must, hide the sale items. This calls for ruthlessness!

- Have a friend assist you in deciding what you can do without. An impartial friend can help you overcome sentimentality when it interferes with your better judgement.

- Consider selling items you want to replace. At first thought you might not consider selling your dining room set even though you had planned on replacing it someday. Consider that you can decide on offering it for a price that would make it worth selling. You may be on your way to getting the new set you wanted. We've included **Ask Us About _____.** ◆ signs to alert Garage Sailors to merchandise that isn't on display.

- Notify your family and friends that you are collecting goods to sell. They may want to join you in conducting the sale, or give you items to sell for them. You may also simply suggest that if you help them clean up and sort through their basement or attic, could you have the unwanted goods for your sale?

- Kids will enthusiastically relinquish their old toys if they are able to sell them at their own booth. We've included a **Toy Sale** ◆ sign that they can post at places where other children and their parents are likely to see them. Good places to hang such signs might be the children's section of the local library or the neighborhood recreational center or playground.

What should I really get rid of?

I haven't used these in years:

This is the kid stuff that should be sold:

I haven't worn these in over a year:

- Imagine closets full of breathing room with only up-to-date garments that fit. Get rid of anything that wasn't worn during the last season for which it was appropriate.

- Look at all of the surfaces of your home. Eliminate dust catchers that you don't absolutely love. If they have sentimental value, you may want to offer them to your children or other relatives before selling. Don't let sentimentality dictate your environment. You may be saving items for others that they have no interest in.

- Regretfully, we suggest that you avoid selling the hideous wedding gift your mother-in-law gave you if she is planning to be there. Otherwise, go for it.

A "Dump Your Junk" Party

The gathering of items for the sale can be fun if it is approached with a playful attitude. For example, before the sale invite your friends to a "dump your junk" party in which they bring an article of clothing or knickknack they don't use to contribute to the sale. Ask each person to select one special item that they really want to get rid of but keep for some curious reason. Ask each person to tell the story about that garment or item. You'll be amazed at the stories people tell.

Recheck the Day Before

The day before your sale we recommend that you recheck your household for items you may have overlooked the first time. Remember, you can always price the item high enough to make the sale worthwhile. Take full advantage of your investment in advertising and time to get rid of everything you can and make as much money as possible.

GARAGE SALE

Some people find holding Garage Sales so fun and profitable that they actually purchase items they suspect will sell for more money and look for such items on a regular basis. More than a handful of individuals have turned successful Garage Sales into businesses as they become specialists in resale, antiques, estate sales or conducting sales or auctions for others. We'd recommend that you conduct several sales before you consider making such purchases. However, we encourage anyone who is truly committed to take their talents and insights as far as they will take them. If you find that you are a budding entrepreneur you'll need to seek more information than is provided here on the legal and tax consequences of resale as an ongoing business.

Important
Make sure to keep an eye out for potentially valuable collectibles as you gather your items to sell. While you probably won't find any hidden treasures in your linen closet, be aware as you're cleaning out the attic or the curio cabinet. Don't sell limited edition plates until you've checked out their value. Don't sell grandma's table, Aunt Emily's costume jewelry, or your father's stamp collection without a good idea of the fair market value. If you're not sure, go to the library and look it up or get an appraisal. We urge you to be careful or else you may end up selling something valuable for next to nothing.

If the price were right, I'd consider selling:

These people could use some help cleaning out their house, basement, or attic:

Preparing Items for Sale

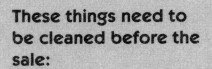

These things need to be cleaned before the sale:

Cleaning and Repairing

Cleaning up your wares before offering them for sale is one of the most important things you can do to increase your sale of goods. A little time and energy invested in cleaning your goods can make them infinitely more appealing, and hence eminently more saleable.

Kitchen utensils are good sellers, but only if they have recently met with a scouring pad. Not everything that is broken needs to be mended, but a little cleaning can go a long way in increasing an item's value and appeal. Here are some pointers:

- Carry out repairs when they enhance the value of an item more than the cost of your time, energy and materials.

- Launder clothes and linens to make them fresh. Leave the ironing to the buyer. Dry cleaning will seldom result in a return on your investment.

- If it is supposed to shine, make it shine.

- If an item consists of several parts, make sure that they are put together in some manner for display. This will make it clear that all the parts are together. Plastic bags, boxes and masking tape can all be used to keep things together.

GARAGE SALE

After cleaning, items will need to be marked. Test electrical appliances and mark each item with the **It Works** and **Doesn't Work** ◆ tags provided in this kit. If you have a puzzle that you know is missing some pieces, make a sticker saying "missing pieces." You can't be expected to know of every scratch on every record, but you shouldn't (and needn't) conceal what you know to be broken. The beauty of garage sale goods is that they have already been broken in.

Do I have old or possibly collectible items I should check the value of?

Pricing items can be a difficult task because there really are no set rules. On the other hand, you need not worry about making mistakes since there are no absolute right or wrong ways of doing it.

The best way of knowing what you can expect an item to sell for is to have visited enough garage sales to get a feel for what things bring. If you don't have much garage sale experience we suggest that you complete the **Pricing Worksheet** ◆ that is included in this kit. This will help you be objective. Remember, our pricing suggestions are only general guidelines.

After completing the worksheet you may want to review it with a friend who has garage sale savvy. Toughen your skin so you won't be offended by your friend's price recommendations, and if you are miles apart in your appraisals, split the difference.

It is all right to give people a bargain. We think that you'll generate more dollar volume if your prices are great. If it sells, even for less than top dollar, you won't miss it, you won't have to handle it again and you'll appreciate the money. If it sells—you win!

General Pricing Guidelines

- The most common benchmark for pricing second hand items (except clothing) is 20% -30% of

GARAGE SALE

their replacement retail value, depending on the condition and desirability of the item. A department store catalog may come in handy for determining retail value. You don't need to find an exact match for the item you are pricing. A similar product of similar quality will do.

- Clothing should be priced much lower. Adult clothing generally brings only 10% of the retail price, but kids clothes can fetch a higher price.

- Don't mistakenly sell a valuable antique. If you have an item you suspect is 100 years old and you are not an antique expert, consult someone who is. To play it safe, if you are uncertain as to the value of an item believed to be 50 years or older, we advise you to store it away until you can determine its value through further investigation. Remember to check all items that might be collectible. The library will have pricing and collectible guides that can be of help.

- When pricing appliances keep in mind that large appliances bought at second hand stores usually include some kind of guarantee. You should never guarantee your goods. The "as is" nature of the sale should be considered in its pricing. We have included a **Bill of Sale** ◆ to be used to transfer ownership of larger or more expensive items. This form specifies that the sale is "as is." If a buyer is pressing you for a guarantee, firmly decline the request. Suggest that they need to determine its condition prior to purchasing the item. You may be able to help them check the fact that it is in working condition by providing an electrical outlet or keeping the washing machine hooked up, etc.

- Knickknacks and like items bought on impulse generally bring less than items that someone has

What current department store catalogs do I have?

What large or valuable items am I selling?

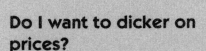

Do I want to dicker on prices?

Will I reduce prices during the sale?

When?

How much?

a practical need to buy, for example, kitchen utensils or appliances.

- Whenever possible group items together and sell on 50¢, $1, or even $2 tables. Even if items are individually priced, it's a good idea. A sign that says **Everything on This Table 10¢ to $1.00** ◆ makes people want to investigate.

Dickering and Discounts

Prices can always be reduced either through haggling or through across the board price reductions near the end of your sale. Haggling is traditional garage sale etiquette, so don't be offended. When someone offers you a sum that you feel is too low you can either: stand firm on your price, dicker with them (giving a counter-offer), or tell them that if they return on the last day, or during the final hours of the sale, prices on remaining items will be reduced.

For many people conducting their first sale, it seems almost rude to be offered 50¢ for an item marked $1, but it helps to realize that Garage Sailors are looking for a bargain and the 50¢ difference will often ensure the item is purchased. A Garage Sale isn't a good time to be rigid or overly sensitive.

If you don't want to dicker, we'd suggest you display our sign saying **Prices Firm As Marked** ◆. If you would prefer to have offers, you might want to display the **Make Us an Offer** ◆ sign to let people know you're willing to dicker.

If you plan on reducing prices at the end of your sale, you may want to post a sign advertising it beforehand (Drastic Price Reductions Beginning Sunday Noon: 30% Off Everything). Or, you may simply hold your tongue until the new prices go into effect (unless pressed to inform hagglers).

Another option is to take written offers. If the haggler insists they can't return for end-of-sale price reductions, record their name, phone number, and offer on an **Offer Card** ◆ and tell them you'll call them if they have offered the highest price by the end of the sale. Taking offers may also be a solution for bigger items for which you want the "best offer." If you do dicker with someone over prices, try to do so as discreetly as possible because everyone within earshot will want to start bargaining with you as well.

The subject of dickering raises another important issue that confronts many holding garage sales: what to do with dealers. In the hours before, or just as your sale begins, you may be visited by someone who is buying things to resell. The common wisdom for handling such people is to tell them to come back at the conclusion of the sale. Beware of letting anyone talk you into "disposing" of your things for you, until you've tried your hand at it.

If you included your phone number in your ad you may hear from dealers before the sale even begins. Including "No Early Birds" in your ad may prevent dealers from visiting before the sale, but if a phone number is included you can't prevent them from calling. This is not the time to make special concessions with dealers. Ask them to call back when the sale is over. After all, they can always join your other customers during scheduled sale hours.

End-of-sale price reductions don't need to include all items if items not included are clearly marked to distinguish them from items which are to be included. If, for example, you want to discount prices 25% from all but a few selected items, give only those selected items a distinguishing mark (for example, an * on the price tag) and post a sign that says **Everything ___% Off! (Except Items Marked with *)** ◆.

How will I handle dealers?

Or, if you are beginning end-of-sale price reductions on a new day, the night before you can put away the items you don't want to reduce and save them for your next sale.

If you are selling items for someone else who will not be at the sale, you should find out what the lowest price they will accept for an item is so you can haggle for them. You should also know whether or not they want their merchandise included in end-of sale price reductions. These issues are clarified in the **Sellers' Agreement ◆**.

Pricing Other People's Merchandise

The owner of the merchandise should arrive at the price—not you. It is okay to offer suggestions on pricing but you want to make certain that the seller understands what the asking price is. If there is no sale at the end of the first day on a substantial item, you may want to suggest a price reduction. However, unless you have a prior agreement, you should not lower the asking price on an item you are selling for someone else.

You should also have a prior agreement with all other sellers about what will be done with their unsold merchandise.

We strongly suggest that you have a written agreement with individuals who are offering merchandise for sale but who will not be working with you during the sale. This **Sellers' Agreement ◆**, specifies the terms under which the merchandise is to be sold, paid for, and removed from the sale. In some cases you will want to charge consignment sellers for some of your advertising expenses and/or charge them a percentage of their proceeds from the sale. These terms should also be put in writing.

Set-up and Display

Set-up and display involves creating the sale environment. It deals with not only arranging goods, but gathering tables and making your refreshment stand. You need to give thought to the set-up and display early in your preparations: at least a week before the sale. While you will probably not actually set-up the sale until the night before and/or the morning it begins, plans need to be laid earlier. Consider each of the following suggestions on set-up and display and use the **Set-up and Display Worksheet** ◆ to compile a list of things you will need to assemble and do.

Refreshment Stand

A refreshment stand is the first thing to consider while thinking about the atmosphere of your sale. Supplying refreshments can make your sale festive and fun, as well as more profitable. You should consider offering free coffee or selling coffee, lemonade, or iced tea.

A Refreshment Stand is a wonderful opportunity for your children (or grandchildren) to participate in your sale and perhaps make money in the process. Help them plan the menu and purchase the supplies. We'd suggest brownies, cookies, sandwiches and drinks. Avoid foods requiring refrigeration.

We've included a **Refreshment** ◆ menu to display the prices of items you are selling. The Refreshment Stand

Should I have a Refreshment Stand?

Do my children know how to make change?

will need its own cash box. Remember to keep track of the amount spent on the food, drinks, plates, cups, ice, napkins, etc. Encourage your kids to determine the profits of their venture by subtracting their expenses and the amount of starting change from their total sales.

Kids Booth

Kids may want to display their goods on separate tables, or even conduct their own mini-sale. They can use our **Toy Sale ◆** signs in conjunction with your garage sale or in conducting their own sale. As with refreshment stands, allowing them to handle their own cash box may be appropriate for older children. A lesson on making change may be required for them to handle this part of the sale effectively.

Garage sales offer children an early experience in doing business and you can include them in every aspect of the planning and execution of the sale.

Cash Station

Of course the most important thing to have at your cash station is change. At a very minimum you need to have $50.00 in change on hand when the sale begins: 15 one dollar bills, 4 five dollar bills, 1 ten dollar bill and 5 dollars in change. Your cash station should also be equipped with:

- a cash box (an old tackle box or cigar box will do)
- a calculator (especially useful for price reductions)
- **Receipts ◆, Sales Records ◆, Offer Cards** and **Bills of Sale ◆**
- an electrical outlet (or extension cord leading to one)
- bags, boxes and wrapping materials
- a measuring tape for customers to use

Although you need change at the Cash Station, you should not keep significant amounts of money in the cash box. You should remove the extra cash frequently over the course of the day, particularly after a large sale. We'd suggest that you designate a secure place inside your house as a place to keep money during the sale. Do not let others know about your hiding place. Consider making a bank deposit at the end of the first day if possible.

A table is easier for people to locate than someone walking around the sale. Your Cash Station table can also be used to display small valuables such as jewelry or electronic equipment with greater security than at an unattended table. Cash Station attendants should also be equipped with access to an electrical outlet for testing appliances. You may need a long extension cord for this purpose.

The Cash Station table should be placed at a strategic location (for example, the back yard gate, if the sale is in the back yard) to make it easier to keep track of who has paid and who hasn't. A table may also be required if you will be keeping record of sales. (See Record Keeping below).

Your Cash Station is also where purchases are packed for the customer to take home. A common complaint about Garage Sales is that there is seldom any thought to how purchases will be taken home. You can be prepared by saving boxes, plastic or paper shopping bags, and wrapping material such as tissue or newspapers for fragile items such as china, glassware, or lamps. String and tape may also be useful.

If customer traffic is light, we suggest that people get up and move around. Straighten things up a bit. There is nothing stranger than being the only person at a sale where

Who will handle the Cash Station at my sale?

GARAGE SALE

a bunch of people are sitting behind tables staring at your every move.

Larger community sales may benefit from having several roving cashiers who are available to answer questions and generally keep an eye on things. Such cashiers can be identified by wearing **Cashier** ◆ name tags.

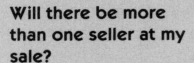

Will there be more than one seller at my sale?

If you have several co-sellers, each with their own items at their own table, you may want each person to handle their own monetary transactions. Even if the merchandise of several sellers is combined, you can solve the problem of elaborate record keeping by having multiple Cash Stations, each identified with a sign: **Pay for Red Tags Here**, or **Pay for Green Tags Here** ◆. You'll need to make sure each seller has their own color and uses it on their own items. This way everyone takes care of their own sales.

Record Keeping

Records can be useful for keeping track of both expenditures and receipts. If you are sharing sale expenses with others you will want to keep track of what you spend. We hope you'll use our **Expense Record** ◆ form to help you.

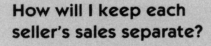

How will I keep each seller's sales separate?

If you are selling the items of several sellers with a single Cash Station, you will want to keep a record of all sales with separate columns for each owner. You will still need to have the merchandise tagged with different colors. We have provided a **Sales Record** ◆ form to help you. Here's the basic approach:

- Divide the merchandise according to color tags.

- Generate a subtotal for each color on the left side of each column.

- Record and total the subtotals on the left side of the Total Sales column (far right column) to

figure the amount each purchaser should pay.

- Collect the money.

- Record each subtotal on the right side of the column.

- Figure the grand totals by adding the figures on the right side of the columns. This way you can keep a running total as the sale progresses.

Here's a sample of two such transactions:

Red		Blue		Total Sales:	
(running total)		(running total)		(running total)	
2.50		5.00		16.00	
12.00		.25		6.75	
1.00		1.50		22.75	22.75
.50		6.75	6.75		
16.00	16.00				
9.00		15.00		9.50	
.50		1.00		16.25	
9.50	9.50	.25		25.75	25.75
	25.50	16.25	16.25		48.50
			23.00		

It is important that the cashier understand the system you are using and be capable of using it properly. (There could be bad feelings on the part of your co-sellers if sales aren't recorded accurately.) You may want to do this function yourself or give it to someone trustworthy. This is probably not a job for one of the kids.

Allow time to go over the procedures with your Cashier before the sale. We recommend a back-up cashier even if you are doing the job. After all, everyone will need to take an occasional break and there may be busy periods—particularly early in the day.

Who will be the back-up Cashier?

Bathrooms and Dressing Rooms

Can I create a Dressing Room?

If you will allow people to use your bathroom, or want to provide someplace for them to try on clothes, you need to decide how you'll arrange for it. They will ask. Security is a concern if you let people wander around your house. You could have someone accompany a shopper through the house to the bath/dressing room and then back to the sale, but it's not likely that you'll want to spare the helpers. Just because you are conducting a public sale on the premises is no reason you should feel obligated to provide these additional services.

If you have lots of clothing to sell you may want to make it more inviting for the buyer by creating a dressing area. If you are holding your sale in or near a garage, you may be able to screen off a corner with sheets or an old shower curtain as a dressing room. We've included a **Dressing Room ◆** sign to hang. A large mirror might be appreciated as well.

What's my policy about customers using the bathroom during the sale?

Under no circumstances should you allow people to enter your home unaccompanied! Even with an escort, allow no more than one person at a time—and you don't even have to permit that. The one person rule includes friends or relatives of the person using the bathroom.

One favorite rip-off scam is for a small group of family members to enter a house together and then begin to rave about the decorating while racing around from room to room calling to each other to look at this or that. Before the unwitting home owner knows it, they've managed to clear out the jewelry box in each bedroom while the owner is glowing from all the flattering attention.

Displaying Clothing

Common garage sale wisdom holds that clothing is not very profitable garage sale merchandise. It brings a lower price, and moves more slowly than other items.

The reason for clothing's bad rap is that people don't take the time to properly display it. A box filled with tools or kitchen utensils inspires people to dig and search; a box of clothes just isn't that interesting and nobody will bother.

However, people will look at your clothes if they don't have to look through them. Display wearing apparel so that they can be examined with minimal handling. The ideal way to do this is by hanging everything on a rack or line. You can display a number of garments by hooking their hangers along the top of a wooden or chain link fence.

Clothing racks can be rented from many equipment or party rental businesses and may be a good investment if you have many quality garments to sell. Clothes pins can be used to attach articles like scarfs, socks and belts to the line (or on hangers for rack). Linens will also display better if hung, but if they are to be arranged on tables, neatly fold them and avoid stacking them in piles.

Related Items with the Same Price

If you have a quantity of similar items (like spools of thread or miscellaneous silverware) place each category of item in a flat box and mark their price on the box, for example, **Everything in this Box 10¢ ◆**. The cashier can be given a price list for these items.

Unrelated Items with the Same Price

Groups of unrelated items can also be sold for the same price if they are assembled on a table marked **Everything on This Table 50¢ ◆**. If the cashier can't be expected to know the contents of the 50¢ table (or can't distinguish them from items on the 25¢ table), then you may either post someone at those tables who will individually mark items for customers who pick up things on those tables, or simply trust the honesty (and memory) of your customers. If you aren't using colored stickers for anything else, you can price code all of the items on a specific table with a particular color. To leave the cashier with a list of all the items on these tables would defeat the purpose of not having to mark each item individually.

Display Tables

You will probably need several tables for displaying merchandise. Folding tables of any kind are extremely useful but you may want to mark them not for sale. In fact, you may want to label anything that isn't for sale from your picnic table to the garden hose with the **Not For Sale ◆** signs we've provided. Try to estimate what tables you'll need and if you don't have enough, borrow them from neighbors and friends. Consider rentals as a possible source if you aren't able to borrow enough.

It is common practice for co-sellers to bring their own tables. This approach certainly can make your life easier.

Display Cases

You can make your own display case for jewelry and other small items of value. Drape a flat box or drawer with dark fabric and cover it with glass or plexiglass. If glass has sharp edges, cover edges with electrical tape or use an empty picture frame.

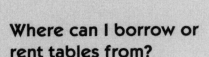

Where can I borrow or rent tables from?

What items should I label "Not for Sale?"

How will I display small valuables?

Remember, security for valuables is one of the reasons for using display cases. This does not mean that you should leave your display case should be left unattended.

Floor Plan

There are two philosophies on arranging garage sale wares. The first is to mix items up, the second is to put all like items together: kitchen things, tools etc. There are also two minds on what to do when your sale thins out. Some people advise rearranging remaining items so that everything is together. Others believe that 'holes' are a sign of a sale worth picking over. We don't believe any of these options make a lot of difference in overall sales. Do whatever you like.

Banners & Decorations

There are lots of ways banners can be used to jazz up your sale and making them can be a fun project for kids. Making them is amazingly easy on many computers or with markers on strips of fabric or old sheets. Use banners for the Refreshment Stand, Kids Booth, Cashier Table, End-of-Sale price reductions, etc. If you aren't up for organizing such creative projects, we've included signs for most of these things.

Use balloons and crepe paper to create a festive atmosphere. Decorating is another fun project for kids.

Name Tags

Name Tags ◆ that identify your Garage Sale Helpers and Cashier make things friendlier. Introducing yourself is a nice touch too. You may have an opportunity to meet neighbors you've never met before.

How will I decorate my sale?

What will I do with my pet during the sale?

Pets

If you think your dog may cause problems on the day of the sale, make arrangements for it to stay somewhere else. Even if you think your pet won't create a problem, you may want to have it out of sight for the day to prevent customer anxiety over allergies or biting. A dog barking or growling in the background doesn't contribute much to your buyer's enjoyment. You may know that it is all bluff, but they don't. So, if your pet is likely to spend the day throwing itself at your back door and barking until it is hoarse, make other arrangements—for your pet's sake if not for your customers.

Rentals

Some of the items you will need to set up your sale can be rented from rental companies. Clothes racks, tables, and even large tents can easily be obtained from these companies. Use your local yellow pages to check the prices of businesses in your area. Many rental businesses include pick up and delivery as part of their service.

Security

The best deterrent is to have several 'garage sale officials' at your sale. It is usually the absence of on-lookers that invites trouble. Make sure you have a sufficient number of helpers and be prepared for people to come in waves instead of evenly dispersed groups throughout the day.

You should take the precaution of locking your house if no one will be inside it. Let the cashier handle the keys so that other helpers will know where to find them. Don't allow customers to enter your home unattended. Don't allow more than one person to enter your home, even if attended. You aren't obligated to provide bathrooms, dressing rooms, or telephones to customers. The safest bet is not to allow any customer to enter your home for any reason.

After the Sale

At the end of the sale, make sure you thank all of the people who have helped you. A small gift is also thoughtful.

Please remove your signs as soon as possible.

Return any tables or other display items you borrowed.

Follow-up on your offer cards. Count your cash, record the amount and deposit it. You will now be able to complete your record keeping. After you've totalled your expenses and deducted the money owed to any co-sellers, you'll be able to calculate the proceeds of the sale.

Notify co-sellers of any unsold items and request they be picked up. Pay your co-sellers for the items that were sold.

Getting Rid of Unsold Items

Some frequent Garage Sale givers keep unsold merchandise to offer at their next sale. Unless you have such a plan, we suggest you call a charitable organization that accepts used goods, like Amvets, the Salvation Army or Goodwill. Most will pick up donations at your door. You may want to pre-arrange a pick-up for the day following your Garage Sale.

Don't give away the items of other sellers unless you have a prior agreement with them to do so.

What will I do with unsold items?

What worked about my Garage Sale?

How Did It Go?

We hope that you are pleased with the amount of money you've made. You've earned it. We also hope you are pleased with the other aspects of the sale. Did you have a good time? Were you well prepared? Did you have enough help? Did your family participate? Did your ads get good response? Did the materials provided here make a difference?

We'd appreciate knowing how your sale went and hearing any ideas you have for improving future editions of this kit. At the back of this book you'll find reply information you can use to write us. We look forward to hearing your stories and thank you in advance for your feedback.

What didn't work about my Garage Sale?

Appendix

Use the following worksheets and signs listed below to plan and execute your own money-making garage sale. To the left of each sign is a brief description of how it can be used and the page number of where the subject is discussed in the text.

The signs, flyers, and invitations are meant to be photo-copied. You can go to your local office supply store or print shop and get copies made for a reasonable price. You may even want to enlarge a few signs. Many copy shops can enlarge on their copiers.

We recommend using brightly-colored or even neon paper because it is much more eye-catching and fun than plain white paper.

Worksheets

Planning Worksheet
Invitation Worksheet
Collecting Worksheet
Advertising Worksheet
Pricing Worksheet
Sign Placement Worksheet
Set-Up Worksheet

Forms

Expense Record
Sales Record
Seller's Agreement
Ad Placement Request
Receipt Forms
Bill of Sale Forms

Invitations & Flyers

Invitations
Flyers

Signs & Tags

Name Tags
Works / Doesn't Work / Not for Sale Tags
Offer Cards / Sold Tags
Cashier Signs
Everything on this: table, rack, box Tags
Make Us an Offer Sign
Prices Are Firm Sign
Dressing Room / No Dressing Room Signs
Kid's Stuff, Cashier, No Smoking Signs
Everything __% Off! Sign
Everything __% Off! Except for items marked * Sign
Ask Us About _____ Sign
Traffic Direction Arrows
No Parking / Park Here Signs
Refreshment Sign
Join Us in the Backyard Sign
Toy Sale Sign
Rained Out Sign
Sales Begins at _____. Please Don't Ring! Sign
Closed—Come Back Tomorrow Sign
Closed Sign
Garage Sale Right Here Sign
Blank Garage Sale Sign

Planning Worksheet

	Invitations & Helpers	Collecting & Display	Advertising & Signs
Before the Sale	☐ Complete Invitation Worksheet ☐ Notify neighbors ☐ Invite people to co-sell and help ☐ Prepare flyers ☐ Distribute flyers ☐ Invite people to attend ☐ Assign color to co-sellers ☐ Complete Sellers Agreements ☐ Review helper schedule ☐ Confirm co-sellers & helpers ☐ Plan lunch for helpers	☐ Collect boxes ☐ Complete Collection Worksheet ☐ Complete Pricing Worksheet ☐ Price items ☐ Clean sale items ☐ Sticker or tag items ☐ Collect supplies needed ☐ Final check for sale items ☐ Arrange for tables & racks ☐ Locate or make display case ☐ Create banners ☐ Collect Cashier Station materials ☐ Make name tags ☐ Photo copy forms or signs ☐ Complete Set-up Worksheet ☐ Review notes in this book	☐ Set sale dates ☐ Set rain dates ☐ Plan location ☐ Apply for permit ☐ Decide where to advertise ☐ Get ad rates & deadlines ☐ Complete Advertising Worksheet ☐ Write ads ☐ Submit ads to papers ☐ Complete Sign Placement Worksheet ☐ Put up Garage Sale signs
Setting-up the Sale	☐ Review Cashier procedures	☐ Set up sale ☐ Arrange sale items ☐ Make pet arrangements ☐ Re-check Set-up Worksheet	☐ Put arrows on signs ☐ Put up parking signs ☐ Put up Sale Begins... sign on door
During the Sale		☐ Lock the house	
After the Sale	☐ Pay the co-sellers ☐ Thank the helpers ☐ Deposit the proceeds	☐ Return borrowed items ☐ Tell us how it went—Thanks!	☐ Remove signs

Invitation Worksheet

Mark the boxes next to the names as shown to indicate the status of your invitation.

    ☑   I *will* invite this person to:

    ☒   I *have* invited this person to:

    ⊗   I've confirmed this person will:

Attend the sale   Join as a co-seller   Bring items to sell   Help out

(Name)

Be sure to include:

Family Members
Friends
Neighbors
Co-workers
Church/Temple Members
Club & Organization Members

Co-seller color assignments:

Red _____
Blue _____
Green _____
Purple _____
Orange _____
Pink _____
(Black is reserved for you)

Help schedule:

Day 1
Morning

_____
_____
_____

Afternoon

_____
_____
_____

Day 2
Morning

_____
_____

Afternoon

_____
_____

Collecting Worksheet

Check your home from top to bottom for items to sell.
We suggest you check a second time just before the sale.

Checked	Re-checked			Checked	Re-checked	
☐	☐	**Attic**		☐	☐	**Kitchen**
☐	☐	**Bedroom #1** _____		☐	☐	**Cabinets**
☐	☐	Closets		☐	☐	**Pantry**
☐	☐	Dressers		☐	☐	**Closet**
☐	☐	**Bedroom #2** _____		☐	☐	**Basement**
☐	☐	Closets		☐	☐	**Laundry**
☐	☐	Dressers		☐	☐	**Office**
☐	☐	**Bedroom #3** _____		☐	☐	**Tools**
☐	☐	Closets		☐	☐	**Sewing Room**
☐	☐	Dressers		☐	☐	**Garage**
☐	☐	**Bedroom #4** _____		☐	☐	**Cedar Closet**
☐	☐	Closets		☐	☐	**Garment Bags**
☐	☐	Dressers		☐	☐	**Storage Locker/Shed**
☐	☐	**Hall Closet #1**		☐	☐	**Toy Box**
☐	☐	**Hall Closet #2**		☐	☐	**Book Shelves**
☐	☐	**Coat Closet**		☐	☐	**Sports Equipment**
☐	☐	**Bathroom #1**		☐	☐	**Bicycles**
☐	☐	Linen Closet		☐	☐	**Records/Tapes/Video**
☐	☐	Sink Cabinet		☐	☐	**Vehicles/trunks**
☐	☐	Medicine Cabinet		☐	☐	**Garage**
☐	☐	**Bathroom #2**		☐	☐	**Crawl Space**
☐	☐	Linen Closet		☐	☐	**Surfaces**
☐	☐	Sink Cabinet		☐	☐	**Walls**
☐	☐	Medicine Cabinet		☐	☐	_____
☐	☐	**Living Room**		☐	☐	_____
☐	☐	Shelves		☐	☐	_____
☐	☐	**Dining Room**		☐	☐	_____
☐	☐	**Den/Family Room**		☐	☐	_____
☐	☐	Shelves		☐	☐	_____

Advertising Worksheet

This worksheet is designed to help you plan your ads and write effective advertising copy. Please refer to the chapter on advertising for additional help.

Sale Information

Sale Dates _____

Rain Dates _____

Sale Times _____

Sale Address _____

_____

Phone Number_____

List of Best Sellers

☐ furniture
☐ books
☐ carpets, rugs
☐ kitchen items
☐ glassware, pottery and dishes
☐ toys
☐ kids clothes
☐ baby equipment and furniture
☐ tools
☐ camping equipment
☐ sports equipment
☐ plants
☐ lamps
☐ vintage jewelry
☐ lamp shades
☐ towels and linens
☐ blankets
☐ picture frames
☐ office and school supplies

Daily Newspaper:_____

Phone _____

Rate per word or line (# of characters per line)

_____

Category or heading _____

Dates to run _____

Deadline for placement_____

Date ad placed _____

Spoke with _____

Weekly Newspaper:_____

Phone _____

Rate per word or line (# of characters per line)

_____

Category or heading _____

Dates to run _____

Deadline for placement_____

Date ad placed _____

Spoke with _____

Shopper:_____

Phone _____

Rate per word or line (# of characters per line)

_____

Category or heading _____

Dates to run _____

Deadline for placement_____

Date ad placed _____

Spoke with _____

Write ad here:

of words or characters

_____ _____

(Write the hook first)

_____ _____

(List the best sellers you have to sell)

_____ _____

_____ _____

_____ _____

_____ _____

(Sale information including dates, times and address)

_____ _____

Total # of words or characters _____

Pricing Worksheet

We recommend that you price most items between 20–30% of the replacement retail price depending on its desirability and condition. Use department store catalogs to determine a replacement retail price for the item. (Find a similar item of a similar quality.) Note: These are general pricing *guidelines* and do *not* apply for collectible items.

Use a calculator to determine your price. For example:

General merchandise
  Excellent condition   Multiply retail price x .3   (30%)
  Good condition   Multiply retail price x .25   (25%)
  Fair condition   Multiply retail price x .2   (20%)

Adult Clothing
  Excellent condition   retail price x .1   (10%)
Kids Clothing
  Excellent condition   retail price x .25   (25%)
  Good condition   retail price x .15   (15%)

Item Name	Retail Price	Percent	My Price

Sign Placement Worksheet

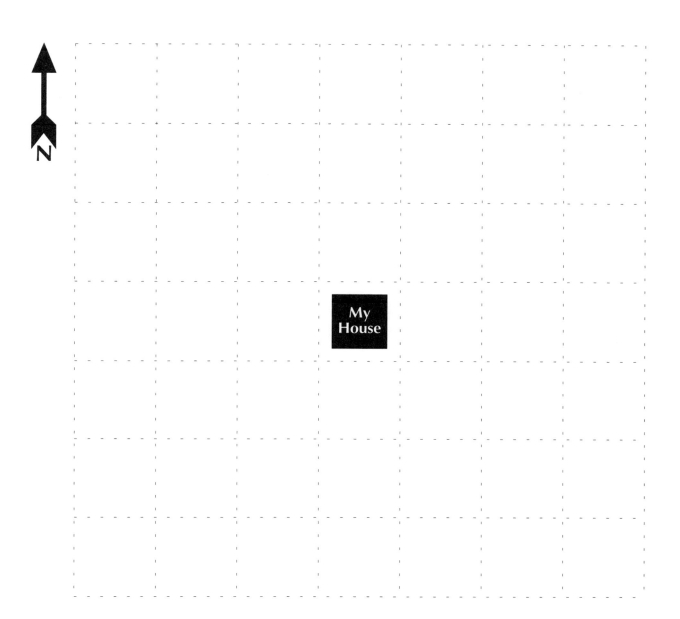

Make sure everyone can find your Garage Sale.

Draw the major streets to the North, South, East and West of your home. (This doesn't have to be to scale.)

Draw the streets that are the most direct route from the major streets TO your house. Avoid any one-way streets that go the wrong direction.

Draw arrows at the major intersections indicating where to turn to get to your house. Remember to put an arrow on each side of the intersection on two-way streets.

Draw arrows to show where any additional turns must be made along each route.

By counting the arrows you now know how many signs and arrows you need and where they should be placed.

Sample Map:

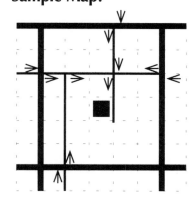

Set-up & Display Worksheet

This worksheet is designed to help you make sure you have all the materials you need for conducting your sale.

Check off the first box when you gather or purchase that item.

Check off the second box to make sure the item is available just before the sale.

General Set-up

- ☐☐ #_____ of tables
- ☐☐ #_____ of chairs
- ☐☐ Banners
- ☐☐ Decorations

Cash Station

- ☐☐ boxes of many sizes
- ☐☐ price stickers and tags
- ☐☐ masking tape
- ☐☐ markers (back-up colors for co-sellers)
- ☐☐ grocery bags
- ☐☐ shopping bags
- ☐☐ extension cord to outlet
- ☐☐ cash box with change
- ☐☐ display case
- ☐☐ tissue
- ☐☐ trash can
- ☐☐ paper towels
- ☐☐ spray window cleaner
- ☐☐ pens
- ☐☐ sun screen
- ☐☐ visor or sun hat
- ☐☐ measuring tape
- ☐☐ Name Tags ◆
- ☐☐ Works/Doesn't Work Tags ◆
- ☐☐ Receipts ◆
- ☐☐ Sales Record ◆
- ☐☐ Bill of Sale ◆
- ☐☐ Offer Cards ◆
- ☐☐ Cashier sign ◆
- ☐☐ Sold signs ◆
- ☐☐ _____
- ☐☐ _____
- ☐☐ _____
- ☐☐ _____
- ☐☐ _____
- ☐☐ _____
- ☐☐ _____
- ☐☐ _____
- ☐☐ _____
- ☐☐ _____

Clothing Display

- ☐☐ price tags
- ☐☐ safety pins (to pin accessories to garments)
- ☐☐ clothing hangers
- ☐☐ clothing rack(s)

Refreshment Stand

- ☐☐ paper cups
- ☐☐ ice
- ☐☐ napkins
- ☐☐ drink mix
- ☐☐ trash can
- ☐☐ cash box
- ☐☐ change
- ☐☐ Refreshments sign ◆

Signs to Display

Check off the first box if you intend to display this sign.
Check off the second box after the sign is displayed.

- ☐☐ Ask Us About _____
  (for items not on display) ◆
- ☐☐ Dressing Room ◆
- ☐☐ Everything in this Box $____ ◆
- ☐☐ Everything on this Rack $____ ◆
- ☐☐ Everything on this Table $____ ◆
- ☐☐ Everything ____% Off!
  (for last day of sale) ◆
- ☐☐ It's in the Back Yard ◆
- ☐☐ Make Us an Offer ◆
- ☐☐ No Parking ◆
- ☐☐ No Smoking ◆
- ☐☐ Not for Sale ◆
- ☐☐ Park Here ◆
- ☐☐ Pay for _____ Tags Here ◆
- ☐☐ Prices Firm as Marked ◆
- ☐☐ Sale Begins at _____. Please Don't Ring. ◆
- ☐☐ Sorry, No Dressing Room ◆
- ☐☐ Toy Sale ◆

Expense Record

This worksheet is designed to help you maintain an accounting of all of the expenses you have in marketing and conducting your sale.

This information will be important if you are sharing the expenses with other sellers. You may want to keep receipts for your expenses as well.

This information is also useful in determining the profitability of your sale.

Areas of Expenses

Permit or License
Advertising
Photocopies
Mailing
Materials & Supplies
Decorations
Rentals
Refreshment Supplies

Date	Expense Item	Amount

Sales Record

Total Sales:

Seller's Name or Color:

Seller's Agreement

Thank you for joining us in the Garage Sale being sponsored by _____.

This form is designed to help plan and organize the sale and assure that everyone knows what to expect. Portions that do not apply can be crossed out.

I will deliver my sale items no later than _____ on _____ and I'll set-up my items for display. I will not hold the sponsor responsible for selling or securing my items.

I will be at the sale during the following times: day _____ time_____

day _____ time_____

My items will be priced as shown on this inventory list and marked with _____ (specify color) labels or markers. Merchandise in boxes or racks to be sold at one price only will be clearly marked/coded.

I will allow the sale sponsor to sell my merchandise for the lowest price shown on this inventory list without seeking additional approval from me.

Please ☐ include / ☐ exclude my items from the end of sale price reduction of _____%.

☐ I will bring my own table and chairs.   ☐ I will need to rent a table and chairs.

I will contribute _____ (specify the dollar amount or percentage of expenses)

towards the expenses of the sale which are estimated to be $_____.

I will pay the sponsor a consignment fee of _____ % of my sale proceeds to defer expenses.

☐ I will pick up my unsold merchandise on _____ (day) _____ (time).
☐ Please donate my unsold items to a charity of the sponsor's choice.

_____   _____   _____
(date)   seller's name   signature

Inventory	My Tag Price/Color	My Lowest Price
_____	_____	_____
_____	_____	_____
_____	_____	_____
_____	_____	_____
_____	_____	_____
_____	_____	_____
_____	_____	_____
_____	_____	_____
_____	_____	_____
_____	_____	_____
_____	_____	_____
_____	_____	_____
_____	_____	_____
_____	_____	_____

(continue on back if needed)

Ad Placement Request

(page 21)

After completing the Advertising Worksheet, write the finished copy for your ad on these forms and fill out the needed information. Send the forms in or drop off your order at your local newspaper.

Classified Ad

Please run the following ad copy from _____ to _____ under **Garage Sales**.

....

....

....

....

☐ Please send billing to:
Name_____
Address_____
City/State/Zip_____
Phone _____

☐ Please charge my _____ account
#_____ Exp _____
signature _____

☐ Payment of $_____ is enclosed.

- -

Classified Ad

Please run the following ad copy from _____ to _____ under **Garage Sales**.

....

....

....

....

☐ Please send billing to:
Name_____
Address_____
City/State/Zip_____
Phone _____

☐ Please charge my _____ account
#_____ Exp _____
signature _____

☐ Payment of $_____ is enclosed.

- -

Classified Ad

Please run the following ad copy from _____ to _____ under **Garage Sales**.

....

....

....

....

☐ Please send billing to:
Name_____
Address_____
City/State/Zip_____
Phone _____

☐ Please charge my _____ account
#_____ Exp _____
signature _____

☐ Payment of $_____ is enclosed.

Receipt Forms

Photocopy additional copies to write out for customers who may wish to have a receipt for their purchases.

GARAGE SALE

Receipt

Date: ....

Name: ....

Item	Amount
Total	

GARAGE SALE

Receipt

Date: ....

Name: ....

Item	Amount
Total	

Bill of Sale

(page 35)

You may want to use a Bill of Sale to transfer ownership of large, expensive, mechanical or electrical items.

GARAGE SALE

Bill of Sale

Seller, _____
                    (seller's name)

of _____
      (address)   (city)   (state)   (zip)

in consideration of _____ dollars,
                            (sale amount)

receipt of which is acknowledged, does hereby sell and transfer

ownership to Buyer, _____
                              (buyer's name)

of _____
      (address)   (city)   (state)   (zip)

the following personal property:

_____
(write a brief description of the sale item)

Seller represents and warrants to Buyer that Seller is the owner of this property and that the property is free and clear of all liens, charges and encumbrances, and that Seller has full right, power and authority to sell said personal property. Seller does not warranty the quality or condition of this property. This property is being sold in "as is" condition.

_____   _____
    (date)   (seller's signature)

GARAGE SALE

Bill of Sale

Seller, _____
                    (seller's name)

of _____
      (address)   (city)   (state)   (zip)

in consideration of _____ dollars,
                            (sale amount)

receipt of which is acknowledged, does hereby sell and transfer

ownership to Buyer, _____
                              (buyer's name)

of _____
      (address)   (city)   (state)   (zip)

the following personal property:

_____
(write a brief description of the sale item)

Seller represents and warrants to Buyer that Seller is the owner of this property and that the property is free and clear of all liens, charges and encumbrances, and that Seller has full right, power and authority to sell said personal property. Seller does not warranty the quality or condition of this property. This property is being sold in "as is" condition.

_____   _____
    (date)   (seller's signature)

Invitations

(pages 11, 13, 21)

Use the Invitation Worksheet to help you determine how many of these you'll want to photocopy. Make some extras too! You may want to fill it out before making copies. Hand invitations to your neighbors, friends, co-workers, etc. Tell them about the fun they'll have and the great bargains they'll find at your Garage Sale.

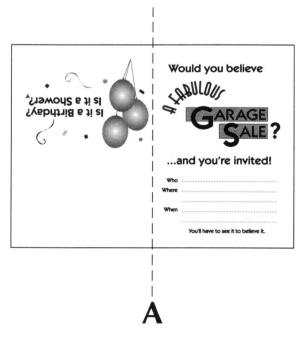

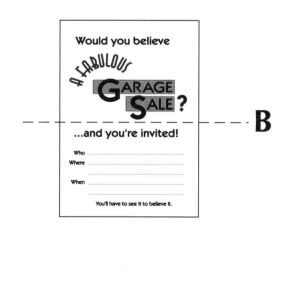

1. Fold in half on line A
   —with the design on the outside.

2. Fold in half again on line B
   —with the balloons on the outside.

Would you believe

FABULOUS

GARAGE SALE?

...and you're invited!

Who ....

Where ....

When ....

You'll have to see it to believe it.

Is it a Birthday?
Is it a Shower?

Flyers

(page 22)

Photocopy enough to post everywhere you go: grocery stores, churches, laundromats, schools, libraries, etc. Remember to check back on your ideas for placing your flyers in the advertising chapter.

IT'S A FABULOUS GARAGE SALE

When: ....

....

Where: ....

....

What's there: ....

....

Name Tags

(page 42)

These name tags are for all of your helpers
to wear during your sale.

Cashier

Cashier

President

May I help?

Security

May I help?

Tags

(page 33)

Attach the appropriate tag to items such as appliances that may or may not work. Use the other tags to identify items you are not selling.

It Works	It Works	It Doesn't Work	It Doesn't Work
It Works	It Works	It Doesn't Work	It Doesn't Work
It Works	It Works	It Doesn't Work	It Doesn't Work
It Works	It Works	It Doesn't Work	It Doesn't Work
It Works	It Works	It Doesn't Work	It Doesn't Work
It Works	It Works	It Doesn't Work	It Doesn't Work
Not For Sale	Not For Sale	Not For Sale	Not For Sale
Not For Sale	Not For Sale	Not For Sale	Not For Sale
Not For Sale	Not For Sale	Not For Sale	Not For Sale
Not For Sale	Not For Sale	Not For Sale	Not For Sale
Not For Sale	Not For Sale	Not For Sale	Not For Sale
Not For Sale	Not For Sale	Not For Sale	Not For Sale

Offer & Sold Cards

(pages 37 & 40)

Offer Card

I'd like to make an offer of

$ _____

For this item:

_____

Name_____

Address _____

Day Phone _____

Evening Phone _____

Offer Card

I'd like to make an offer of

$ _____

For this item:

_____

Name_____

Address _____

Day Phone _____

Evening Phone _____

Offer Card

I'd like to make an offer of

$ _____

For this item:

_____

Name_____

Address _____

Day Phone _____

Evening Phone _____

Offer Card

I'd like to make an offer of

$ _____

For this item:

_____

Name_____

Address _____

Day Phone _____

Evening Phone _____

Sold

Payment must be made in full.

Item will be picked up:

_____

Name_____

Address _____

Day Phone _____

Evening Phone _____

Sold

Payment must be made in full.

Item will be picked up:

_____

Name_____

Address _____

Day Phone _____

Evening Phone _____

Sold

Payment must be made in full.

Item will be picked up:

_____

Name_____

Address _____

Day Phone _____

Evening Phone _____

Sold

Payment must be made in full.

Item will be picked up:

_____

Name_____

Address _____

Day Phone _____

Evening Phone _____

Cashier

(page 42)

Fill in the color of your co-sellers merchandise to be paid for at a separate cashier.

Everything on this Table

→

(pages 24, 37, 45)

Photocopy if you need additional signs to price a whole table, rack or box of items. For example, "Everything on This Table $1" or "Everything in This Box 50¢."

Everything on this Table

Everything on this Table

Everything on this Rack

Everything on this Rack

Everything in this Box

Everything in this Box

Make Us an Offer

→

(pages 36, 37)

Display this sign if you are willing to dicker on prices.

GARAGE SALE

Make us an Offer.

Prices are Firm

➤━━━━━━━━━━━━━━━━━━➤

(pages 36, 37)

Display this sign if you are not willing to dicker on prices.

GARAGE SALE

Prices are Firm as Marked.

Dressing Room

(page 44)

Display the appropriate sign to let customers know if there is a dressing room.

Dressing Room

Sorry—No Dressing Room

Misc. Signs

Use these signs if you want to separately label kid's stuff, identify a cashier, or if there is no smoking on the premises.

Kid's Stuff

Cashier

Cashier

No Smoking Please

Everything   % Off!

(page 37)

Display this sign to really move items for less. Be ready with a calculator. The bottom can be used to include additional information such as: Beginning Sunday at 2:00.

Everything % Off!

Everything % Off! Except...

(page 37)

Use this sign if some items are to be excluded from additional discounting. Remember to put the star on the tags of the items that are excluded.

Everything __% Off!

(except for items marked with ★)

Ask Us About

➤━━━━━━━━━━━━━━➤

This sign can alert people to sale items that are not on display. For example, your washer and dryer in the basement or your dining room table and chairs which are still in the dining room.

Ask Us About

Traffic Direction Arrows

➤ (arrow pointing right)

(see Sign Placement Worksheet)

Photocopy the arrows and cut them apart.
Glue or tape them on the Garage Sale signs
to help direct people to your sale.

No Parking / Park Here

(page 13)

Post these to help control the traffic
and parking near your home.

GARAGE SALE

No

Parking

GARAGE SALE

Park

Here

Refreshments

→

(page 39)

Use this sign to write a menu of the refeshments you have to offer and their prices. If you are providing complementary beverages, make sure that it is clear to your customers.

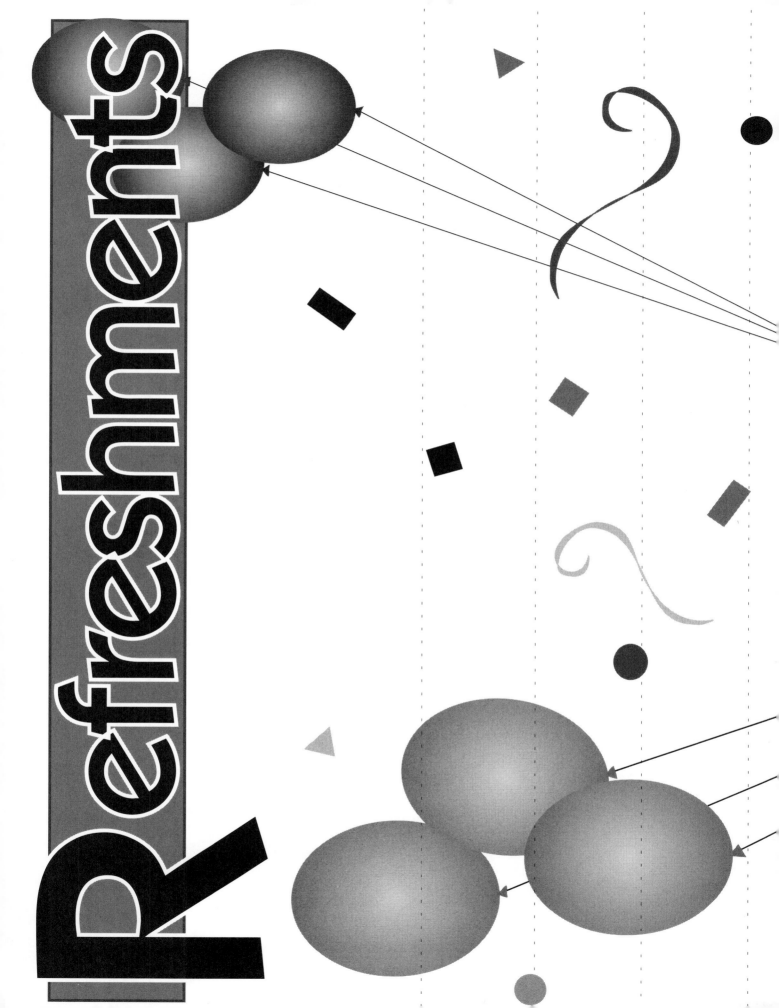

Refreshments

Join us in the back yard.

⟵━━━━━━━━━━━━━━⟶

Fill in the area where your sale is, for example, back yard, front porch, etc. Display this sign on the mail box, front door (wherever it is most visible) to direct your customers to your sale.

GARAGE SALE

Join us

Toy Sale Sign

(pages 29 & 40)

This sign can be used by kids to hold their own sale. Use the bottom lines to show the sale date, time and location and post them where kids (and their parents) are likely to see them. You can also use this sign during a sale to indicate the designated toy area.

TOY SALE

We're Rained Out

⬛➡️

(page 17)

Place this sign on your front door if you get rained out and plan to hold your Garage Sale the following weekend.

Sorry—
We're rained out.

Please come back
next week!

Sale begins at

(page 17)

Write the starting time on the dotted line and post this sign on your front door the night before your sale begins to avoid disturbance from early arrivals.

Closed for the day

(page 17)

Post this sign at the end of your Friday and/or Saturday sale to let late comers know that you'll be open again the next day.

We are closed for the day.

Please come back tomorrow at

We're closed

→

(page 17)

Post this sign at the end of the
last day of your sale.

Right Here!

(page 22)

Display this sign on your front door a couple of weeks before your sale to let everyone passing by know where the location is. Remember to boldly and clearly write in the sale days and times on the bottom line.

GARAGE SALE

Right Here!

Garage Sale Sign

(pages 22-24)

Carefully fill in the dates, times and address of your sale and then photo-copy enough signs to place around your neighborhood. Use the Sign Placement Worksheet to help you determine how many are needed. Use the arrows to help direct people to your home. If you want larger signs, ask your local copy shop to enlarge them for you. Use bright colored paper to attract attention.

GARAGE SALE

Dear Reader,

We hope that this kit helped you plan and execute a successful Garage Sale. We would love to hear about how your sale went—what worked and what didn't. We are sure our other readers would appreciate your tips in future editions of this book.

If you have a few minutes, would you mind jotting down your thoughts and sending them to us? We'd love to know how much you made, how many people showed up and any stories you may have. Were the worksheets helpful? Did you like the signs? Did you have any questions that went unanswered?

If there were a newsletter available for people who enjoy giving and attending Garage Sales would you want to know about it? If so, please make sure to give us your correct name and address. What information would you want to see in such a newsletter?

Does your community, church or charitable organization plan to hold a Garage Sale in the future? Would you recommend this kit to others?

Thank you for the feedback! You can write to us at this address:

The Garage Sale Sisters
c/o The Print Group
2835 N. Sheffield, St. 200
Chicago, IL 60657

Happy Garage Sailing,

Diana Rix & Monica Rix Paxson

SMALL BUSINESS SOURCEBOOKS
The books designed to help you grow your business.

Your First Business Plan
by Joseph Covello & Brian Hazelgren

Learn the critical steps to writing a winning business plan! *Your First Business Plan* has special tips for new and start-up business owners , tells you which sections of your business plan business lenders are most likely to scrutinize, how to develop your financial projections, and much more! *Your First Business Plan* is written in a simple, step-by-step format and has easy to understand examples of actual business plans.

145 pages ISBN 0-942061-47-0 (hardcover) $17.95

Smart Hiring for Your Business
by Robert Wendover

Smart Hiring shows you how to hire the right employee the first time, and save money, time and headaches. *Smart Hiring* teaches you how to hire the best employees for your business by explaining all of the issues involved in the hiring process. You'll get checklists for each step of the process , including: • Hiring Laws •Recruiting Basics • Conducting Reference Checks • Job Descriptions & Compensation • Evaluating Resumes • Decision Making Checklist , and more. Don't let poorly recruited staff create unnecessary problems for you and your business. Get *Smart Hiring* and see what having the best employees can do for you and your business.

156 pages ISBN 0-942061-57-8 (hardcover) $17.95

How to Get a Loan or Line of Credit for Your Business
by Bryan E. Milling

A banker shows you exactly what to do to get a loan or line or credit for your business. You'll discover: • how bankers review business loan requests • how to apply for a bank loan • how to increase your chances of getting a loan • how to evaluate and negotiate the loan package your bank is offering, and more. Get a crash course in bank loans with *How to Get a Loan or Line of Credit for Your Business.*

145 pages ISBN 0-942061-46-2 (hardcover) $17.95

How to Market Your Business
by Ian B. Rosengarten, MS, MPH

An introduction to the tools and tactics for marketing your business. You'll get 69 tools to help grow your business, including; • Customer Appreciation Programs • In-Store Displays • Press Releases • Brochures • Customer Surveys, and more. *How to Market Your Business* shows you at a glance, the time, money and professional resources needed to implement different marketing programs for your business. Learn how to put together a mix of programs that will get results with *How to Market Your Business* today!

142 pages ISBN 0-942061-48-9 (hardcover) $17.95

—Sourcebooks will release new books in this series each Fall and Spring. Call Sourcebooks at 1-800-798-2475 for information on the upcoming books in our Small Business Series.

SOURCEBOOKS TRADE—
How-To Books For *Today's* Needs

Cash Flow Problem Solver: Common Problems and Practical Solutions

by Bryan E. Milling

Now in its third edition, *Cash Flow Problem Solver* is a proven best-seller and has helped over 20,000 business owners improve their cash flow and benefit from effective cash flow management. *Cash Flow Problem Solver* provides a results-oriented, step-by-step guide with tools and specific tactics to assure positive cash flow and to help boost a firm's profits. Cited as one of the three books on the "Smart CEO's Reading List" in INC Magazine. Selected as an alternate of both the **Business Week Book Club** and the **Fortune Book Club.**

296 pages ISBN 0-942061-28-4 (hardcover) $32.95

Creating Your Own Future: A Woman's Guide to Retirement Planning

by Judith Martindale, CFP and Mary J. Moses

Winner of the 1992 Mature Media Award for Financial Services.

Retirement planning is especially critical for women because they have unique factors that they need to consider when planning for their retirement. Creating Your Own Future explains why factors such as, shorter work lives due to child rearing, longer life expectancy, differing health needs than men's makes retirement planning for women <u>absolutely</u> essential. "**Highly Recommended**" *Booklist.*

256 pages ISBN 0-942061-08-X (hardcover) $28.95

The Small Business Survival Guide: How To Manage Your Cash, Profits and Taxes

by Robert E. Fleury

The Small Business Survival Guide includes discussions on: • planning for and filing taxes • cash flow analysis and management • understanding and developing financial statements • methods of taking and valuing inventory • how to value a business for buying and selling • managing your payroll & recordkeeping • PLUS...**NO-ENTRY ACCOUNTING...a means of doing and understanding your own accounting, without double-entry bookkeeping.**

256 pages ISBN 0-942061-11-X (hardcover) $29.95

Small Claims Court Without A Lawyer

by W. Kelsea Wilber, Attorney-at-Law

Small Claims Court Without A Lawyer is an invaluable guide to understanding the small claims system. It allows you to file a claim and get a judgement quickly and economically, without an attorney's assistance or fee. Written in clear, uncomplicated language, this useful new book includes details about each state's small claims court system, so that wherever you live you can use it to successfully file a claim and see that claim through to a judgement.

224 pages ISBN 0-942061-32-2 (paperback) $18.95

In 1990, Sourcebooks, Inc., started its trade division, Sourcebooks Trade. Our goal was to provide easy-to-understand, empowering how-to books for today's consumers. We now offer a wide range of expertise in business and finance books, marketing, current affairs, self-help and reference designed to make consumers' lives easier.

To order these books or any of our numerous other publications, **please contact your local bookseller,** or call Sourcebooks at 1-800-798-2475. Get a copy of our catalog by writing or faxing:

Sourcebooks Trade, A Div. of Sourcebooks, Inc.
P.O. Box 372, Naperville, IL 60566
(708) 961-2161   Fax (708) 961-2168

Thank you for your interest in our publications.